Here are the answers to the funnies on the front!

How do you stop a bull from charging?
TAKE AWAY HIS CREDIT CARD!!!

What do you call a man who is wiring for money?
AN ELECTRICIAN!!

What does a 500-pound mouse say?
HERE, PUSSYCAT!!

Why don't many gorillas go to college?
BECAUSE THEY DON'T FINISH HIGH SCHOOL!!

What are nitrates?
USUALLY CHEAPER THAN DAY RATES!!

**Feeling foolish?
Then try the riddles in the middle!**

**Feeling silly? Then try
the laughs at the last!**

**YOU'RE IN FOR FUN ALL THE WAY THROUGH
WITH LOTS OF FUNNY RIDDLES!**

Lots of Funny Riddles

Joseph Kiernan

WARNER BOOKS

A Warner Communications Company

WARNER BOOKS EDITION

Cover design by New Studio

Interior art by Joseph Kiernan

Warner Books, Inc., 75 Rockefeller Plaza, New York, N.Y. 10019

A Warner Communications Company

A Warner Communications Company

Printed in the United States of America

First Printing: August, 1981

10 9 8 7 6 5 4 3 2 1

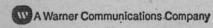

Lots of
Funny
Riddles

What does Count Dracula do every morning at eleven?
He takes a coffin-break.

~~~~~~

Name one school where you have to drop out to graduate.
Parachute school.

What is purple and weighs 3,000 tons?
Moby grape.

~~~~~~

How do you stop a bull from charging?
Take away his credit card.

What occupation do you have to start at the top?
A barber.

~~~~~~

How can you tell when the moon is going broke?
When it's down to its last quarter.

What do you call a man who wires for money?
An electrician.

~~~~~~

How can you tell if a prisoner is rich?
If he has an unlisted number.

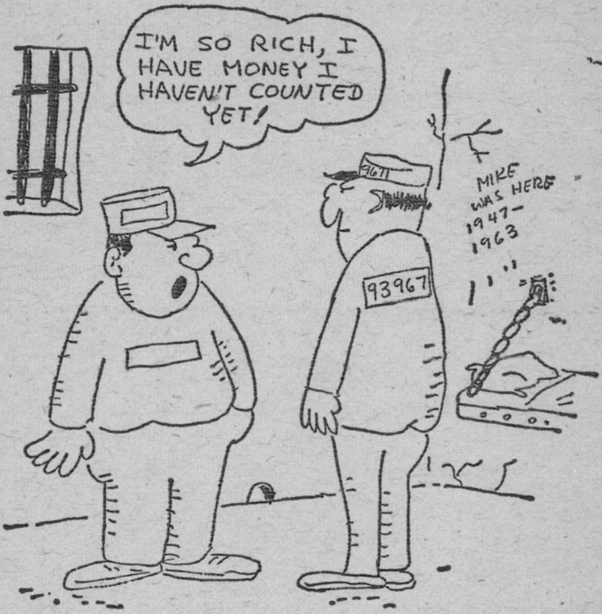
I'M SO RICH, I HAVE MONEY I HAVEN'T COUNTED YET!
93967
MIKE WAS HERE 1947–1963

What man is happy when his business goes to the dogs?
A veterinarian.

~~~~~~

When does a school teacher wear sunglasses?
When she has bright students.

Why do bats fly at night?
Because they can't find their car keys.

~~~~~~

What is yellow and goes rat-atat-tat-tat-tat?
A banana with a machine gun.

What is it that everyone on earth is doing right now?
Growing old.

~~~~~~

What does a 500 pound mouse say?
"Here kitty, here kitty."

What looks exactly like a half of a grapefruit?
The other half.

How do you make a pair of pants last?
Make the jacket and vest first.

Why did the crook take a shower?
To make a clean getaway.

~~~~~~

What famous baseball player wears the biggest cap?
The one with the biggest head.

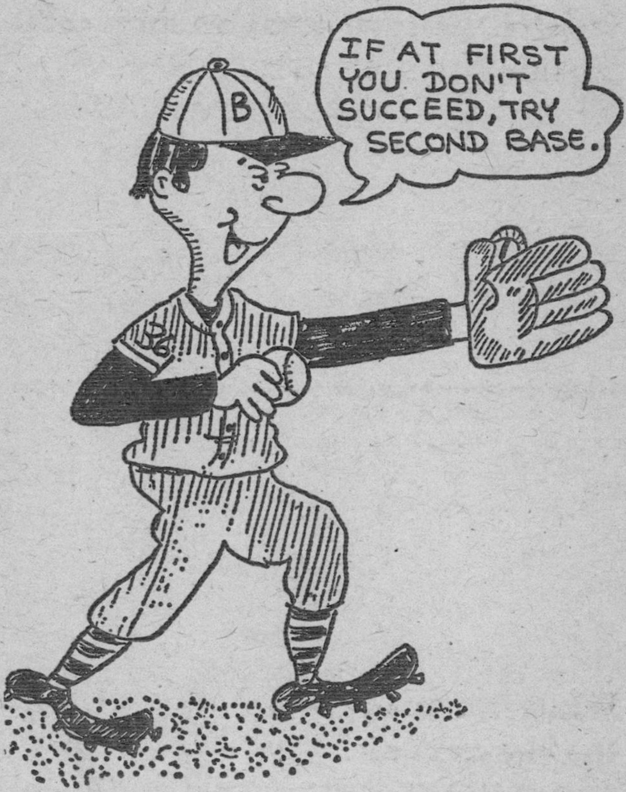
IF AT FIRST YOU DON'T SUCCEED, TRY SECOND BASE.

What's yellow and weighs 350 pounds?
A banana with a thyroid condition.

~~~~~~

Why don't many gorillas go to college?
Because they don't finish high school.

Where do crocodiles put their money?
In a river bank.

~~~~~~

What is worse than a kid playing bagpipes?
Two kids playing bagpipes.

What is the easiest way to catch a fish?
Have someone throw it to you.

~~~~~~

Which is heavier, a ton of gold or a ton of chicken feathers?
They both weigh the same—a ton.

What do you call a ten-foot tall, hairy entertainer?
The Abominable Showman.

~~~~~~~~~~~~~~~~~~~~~~~~~~~~~~~~~~~~~

What are nitrates?
Usually cheaper than day rates.

Why did the man put a four-leaf clover under a steamroller?
He wanted to press his luck.

~~~~~~

What animal keeps time the best?
A watchdog.

What goes up when the rain comes down?
Umbrellas.

~~~~~~

What did the farmer say when the carrot insulted him?
"You're a fresh vegetable."

Who has more lives than a cat?
A frog. He croaks many times a day.

~~~~~~

What did Julius Caesar say when he was stabbed?
"Ouch!!"

How do you make a venetian blind?
Stick a finger in his eye.

~~~~~~~~~~~~~~~~~~~~~~~~~~~~~~~~~~~~~

Were there any big men born in Chicago?
No, only babies.

Why did the boy flood the gym?
Because the basketball coach told him to come in as a sub.

~~~~~~

Why did Frankenstein's monster play cards in the cemetery?
Because he could always dig up another player there.

What is the best way to get something out from under a tiger?
Wait for the tiger to go home.

~~~~~~

What do you get when you mix a jar of peanut butter, a jar of jam, and a jar of honey with the Wolfman?
A sticky monster.

Where do you find China?
In the kitchen cabinet.

~~~~~~

Why did the guy drop out of the bakery school?
Because he didn't have enough dough.

How many sides does a cat have?
Two. The inside and the outside.

~~~~~~

What do you call a small dog who was caught in freezing weather?
A pupsickle.

Two silkworms had a race. Who won?
Neither. They ended up in a tie.

———————————————————

Why do elephants wear dark sunglasses?
They're tired of signing autographs.

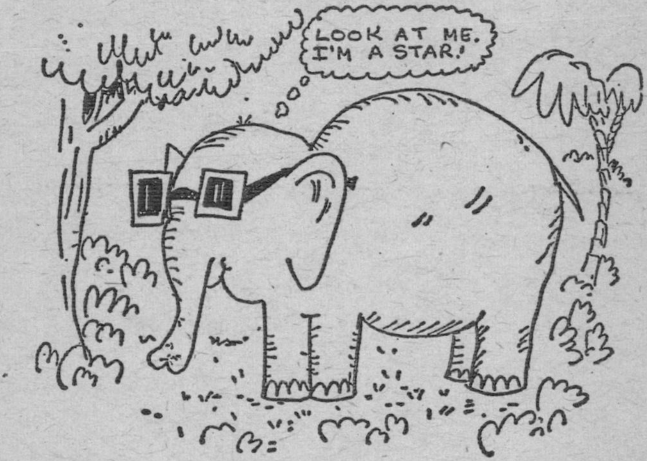
LOOK AT ME.
I'M A STAR!

What do you get if you cross a robin with an elephant?
A five-ton bird that likes peanuts.

~~~~~~

What is a paradox?
Two doctors.

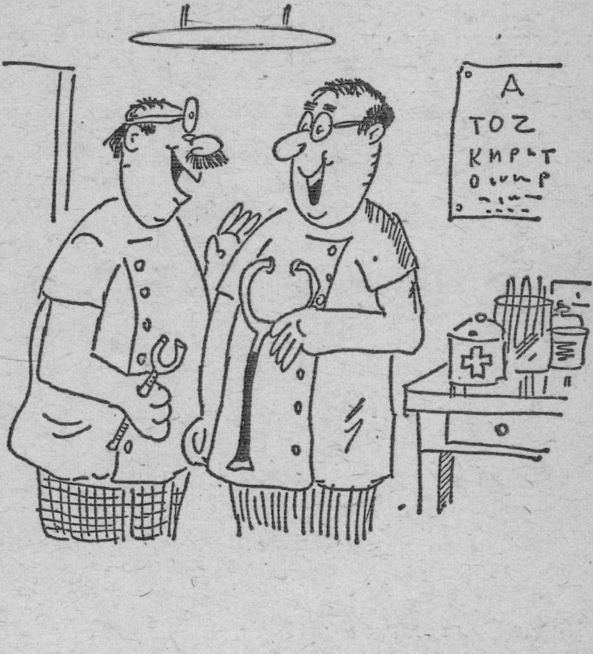
A
TOZ

Why did the kid swallow a stick of dynamite?
Because he wanted to go places.

~~~~~~~~~~~~~~~~~~~~~~~~~~~~~~~~~~~~~

How do boys laugh?
"He, he, he!"

Why is it very dangerous to do math problems in a jungle?
Because if you add 4 and 4, you get 8.

~~~~~~

Why doesn't an elephant ride a bike?
Because he doesn't have a finger to ring the bell.

What number becomes larger when you turn it upside down?
6 turns into 9.

~~~~~~

What bird can you find in your throat?
A swallow.

When is a department store like a boat?
When it has a sale.

~~~~~~

Why do bees hum?
Because they can't remember the words.

What holiday do vampires like the most?
Fangsgiving.

~~~~~~

What do elephants have that no other animals have?
Baby elephants.

How is ink like a pig?
They both can be found in a pen.

~~~~~~

Why is Ireland the richest country in the world?
Because it's capital has been Dublin for many years.

Where does Thursday come before Wednesday?
In the dictionary.

Why didn't the boy like the dictionary?
He found it too wordy.

What has four wheels and flies?
A garbage truck.

~~~~~~~~~~~~~~~~~~~~~~~~~~~~~~~~~~~~~~

What is black and white and red all over?
An embarrassed zebra.

Why was the cannibal thrown out of high school?
Because he was caught buttering up his teacher.

~~~~~~

What is a screen door?
Something kids get a real big bang out of.

What has six legs, two heads and one tail?
A man riding a donkey.

~~~~~~

What has three eyes and blinks alot?
A three-way traffic light.

What is soft and brown and very dangerous?
Shark-infested chocolate pudding.

~~~~~~

What is the best way to start a fire with two sticks?
Be sure one of the sticks is a match stick.

What has no feet, but wears out shoes?
A sidewalk.

~~~~~~

What did one eye say to the other eye?
"Hey, do you live on this block, too?"

Why did the man strike the dentist?
Because he got on his nerves.

~~~~~~

He goes out every single day, but he never leaves his home. Who is he?
A turtle.

What do you get when you cross a
bridge with a car?
Across.

How do you make a slow dog fast?
Don't feed him.

Why did the boy like to play football?
Because he got a kick out of it.

~~~~~~

What animal drives a car?
A road hog.

What did the basketball coach do when he caught the boy shooting baskets?
He took away the kid's rifle.

How does a hotdog speak?
Frankly.

Four men fell into a lake. Why did only three of them get their hair wet?
Because one of them was bald.

~~~~~~

How did the Spanish bullfighter put the bull to sleep?
He used a bulldozer.

What is the difference between an old quarter and a new dime?
Fifteen cents.

~~~~~~

What is green and red and hums alot?
A frog with chicken pox carrying a pet bee.

Why didn't the woman like the taste of her sponge cake?
She said she put too many sponges into it.

~~~~~~

What's yellow and goes putt-putt-putt?
An outboard banana.

What do you get if you cross a gorilla with a parrot?
I don't know, but when it talks you better listen.

~~~~~~

How are a basketball player and a baby alike?
They both dribble alot.

What kind of fish can fix a piano?
A piano tuna.

~~~~~~

Why was the baseball team called the "Dirty Carpets?"
Because they were always getting beaten.

Where is the best place to look for a helping hand?
At the end of your own arm.

Why did they hang the painting?
Because they couldn't find the artist.

Why does a bear sleep for five months?
Who's going to wake him?

───────────────────────────────

What do you call a lazy butcher?
A meat loafer.

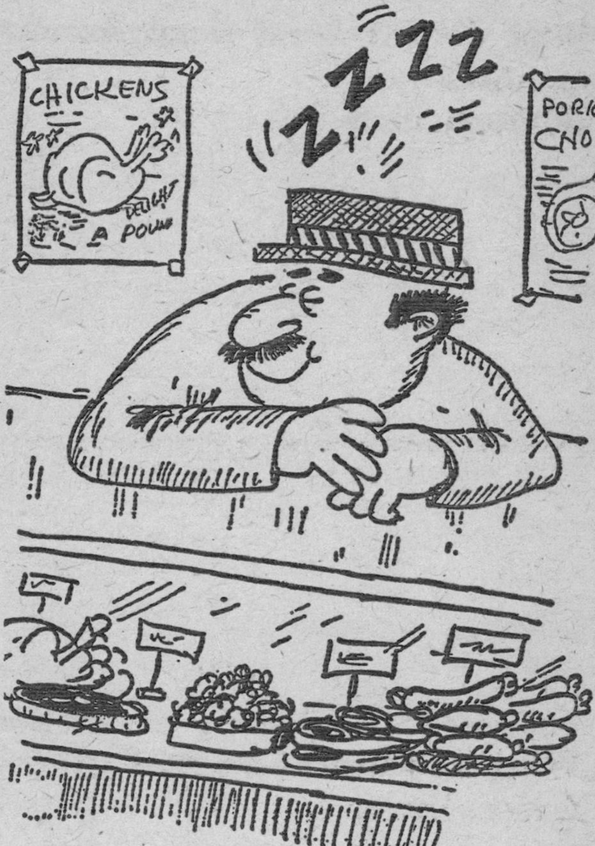
CHICKENS
DELIGHT
ZZZZ
PORK
CHOP

What were the first words from a scientist's baby?
"Mamma, Data."

~~~~~~

What's the difference between a grape and a hippopotamus?
Their color.

What is filled every morning and emptied every night?
A sneaker.

~~~~~~

Are tulips lazy?
Yes—you always find them in bed.

How much milk does the average cow give?
None. You have to take it away from her.

~~~~~~

Why did the kid throw the clock out the window?
He wanted to see time fly.

What did one cat say to the other as they watched a tennis mach? "My Dad is in that racket."

~~~~~~

What's the hardest thing about learning how to skate? The ice when you fall down.

What's round on the ends and high in the middle?
The word Ohio.

How do you make an elephant float?
Two scoops of ice cream, soda, a cherry, and some elephant.

What do you have when a robin flies into a lawn mower?
A shredded tweet.

~~~~~~

How do you make a Chinese egg roll?
Give it a push.

What did Paul Revere say when he walked past a barbershop in London?
"The British are combing."

~~~~~~

What's yellow and blue all over?
A sad banana.

If you have seven apples and six kids, how can you divide them equally?

You make apple sauce.

~~~~~~

What is it that the more you take away, the bigger it becomes?

A hole.

What are two things you can't eat before breakfast?
Lunch and dinner.

~~~~~~

How did the boy break his leg raking leaves?
He fell out of the tree.

Why did the man put his car in the furnace?
He wanted a hotrod.

~~~~~~

How do you catch a rabbit?
You hide between a tree and make a noise like a carrot.

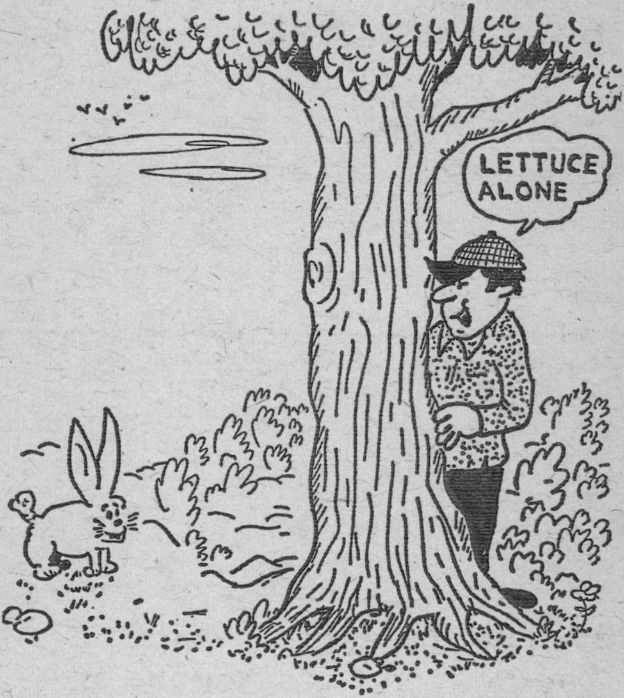
LETTUCE
ALONE

What did the flea do when he be-came rich?
He bought his own dog.

What has many eyes, but can't see?
A potato.

Where was the Declaration of Independence signed?
At the bottom.

~~~~~~

What was the toughest job in the world?
Wheeling, West Virginia.

Why did the Indian ride bareback?
Because his shirt was in the laundry.

~~~~~~

Why did the kid cut a hole in the livingroom rug?
He wanted to see the floor show.

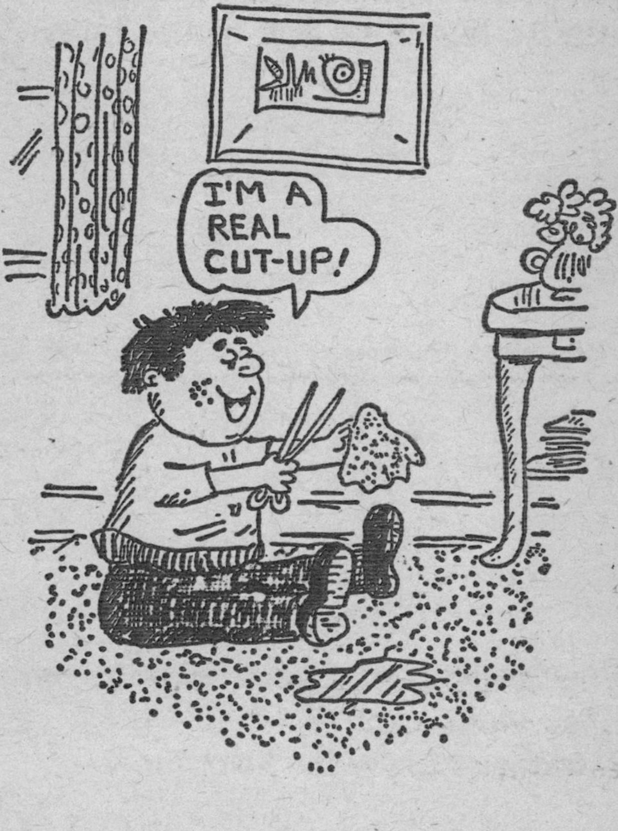
I'M A
REAL
CUT-UP!

Where is Moscow?
Right next to Pa's cow.

***

Seven is an odd number. How can it be made even?
Take away the "s."

What time is it when 15 dogs chase
one cat?
Fifteen after one.

〰〰〰〰〰〰〰〰〰〰〰〰〰〰〰〰〰〰

What goes "snap, crackle, pop?"
A lightning bug with a short cir-
cuit.

Where does a 700 pound gorilla sleep?
Anywhere he wants to.

~~~~~~

Four people are standing under one umbrella. Why don't they get wet?
Because it is not raining.

What did the new suitcase say to the old one?
"You are a sad case."

What is on the dark side of the moon?
Hold-up men.

When is a door not a door?
When it is ajar.

~~~~~~

Why did the boy put bread crumbs in his sister's shoes?
Because he heard she was pigeon-toed.

What's purple and goes click, click, click?
A grape with a camera.

~~~~~~

Why didn't the crazy guy like to go to football games?
Because everytime a team went into a huddle, he thought they were talking about him.

What's a grecian urn?
About ten dollars a day.

~~~~~~

What do you call a man who can turn lead into gold?
A plumber.

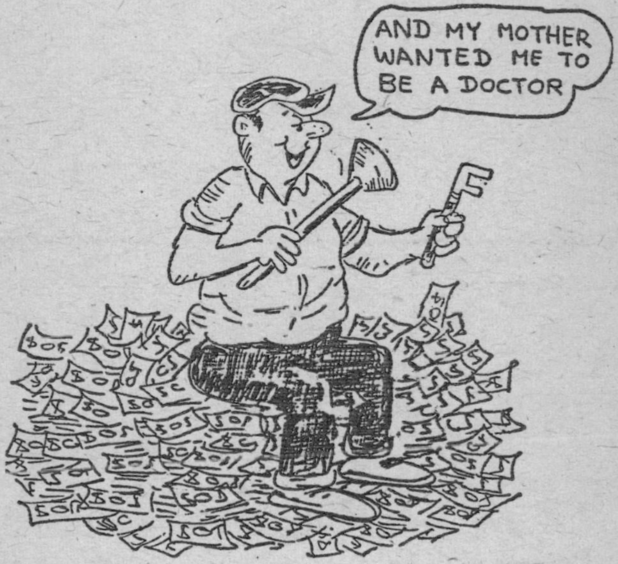
AND MY MOTHER WANTED ME TO BE A DOCTOR

What did the elephant do when he broke his big toe?
He called for a big tow truck.

Why do they have a fence around a graveyard?
Because people are dying to get in.

Why did Frankenstein's monster think Doctor Frankenstein was funny?
Because he kept him in stitches.

~~~~~~

Why are gorillas black?
So you can tell them from canaries.

How do you get an elephant out of a box of cake mix?
Just follow the directions on the back of the box.

~~~~~~

What is a minor operation nowadays?
One that costs less than 2,000 dollars.

What did one horse say to another?
"I don't remember your mane, but your pace is familiar."

∿∿∿∿∿∿∿∿∿∿∿∿∿∿∿∿∿∿∿∿∿∿∿∿∿∿∿∿∿∿∿∿

What kind of dog does Count Dracula have?
A blood hound.

Where were pears first found?
On a tree.

~~~~~~~~~~~~~~~~~~~~~~~~~~~~~~~~~~~~~~~

With which hand should you stir your chocolate soda?
Neither hand. You should use a spoon.

What did the minister say when he saw his church on fire?
"Holy smoke!"

~~~~~~

How can you keep a rooster from crowing on Friday?
Eat him on Thursday.

Why was the ant running on the box of cookies?
Because on the side of the box it read, "Tear along the dotted line."

~~~~~~

Why was the mother kangaroo worried about her son?
Because he didn't feel jumpy late-ly.

Where is the only place you can't walk out on a dull movie?
In an airplane.

~~~~~~~~~~~~~~~~~~~~~~~~~~~~~~~~~~~~

What did the cannibal chef say when he found a pilot in his pot?
"What is this flier doing in my soup?"

What do they call Russians who ride on a train?
Passengers.

~~~~~~~~~~~~~~~~~~~~~~~~~~~~~~~~~~~~~~

If Moby Dick was royalty, what would they call him?
The Prince of Whales.

How did the ghost get into the house?
With a skeleton key.

What is the best way to keep a goat from smelling?
Cut off its nose.

What is green and blue with long sharp red teeth?
I don't know but it's sitting on your shoulder.

~~~~~~~~~~~~~~~~~~~~~~~~~~~~~~~~~~~~~

Why did the teenage boy call his girlfriend "Appendix?"
Because it cost so much to take her out.

Why do they call it a cookbook?
Because it has so many stirring chapters.

Why does a sheep go over a mountain?
Because he can't go under it.

Why did the elephant quit his job
with the circus?
He was tired of working for peanuts.

~~~~~~

What's the best thing to put into a
strawberry short cake?
Your teeth.

Why didn't the mummy, King Tut, have any friends?
Because he was all wrapped up in himself.

~~~~~~

Why did the farmer place razor blades in the ground next to his tomato plants?
Because he wanted his tomato to grow already sliced.

Why was the cat so small?
Because it drank condensed milk.

~~~~~~~~~~~~~~~~~~~~~~~~~~~~~~~~~~~~~~~

Why didn't the cowboy like his ten-gallon hat?
Because he had an eight-gallon head.

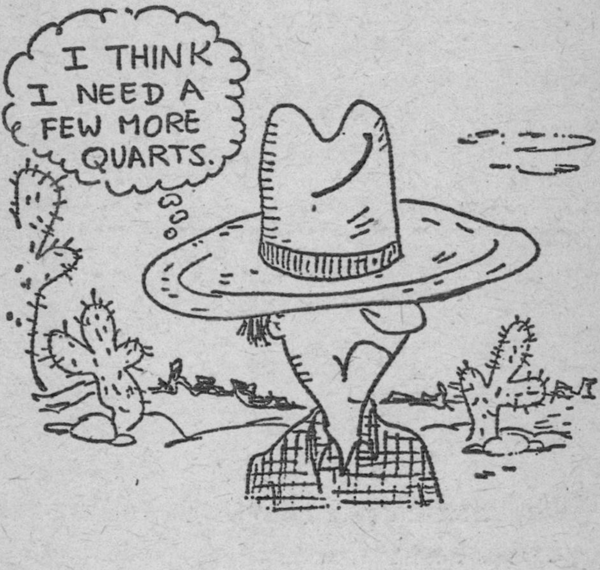
I THINK I NEED A FEW MORE QUARTS.

Where do bugs go in the winter time?
Search me.

~~~~~~

Why won't they let Cinderella play baseball anymore?
Because last night she ran away from the ball.

How do you make a tomato surprise?
Sneak up behind him and go "Booo!!"

~~~~~~

Why is a policeman so strong?
Because he can hold up twenty cars.

What is yellow and goes around and around?
A long-playing omelet.

~~~~~~

How many hotdogs can a man eat on an empty stomach?
Only one. After that his stomach isn't empty anymore.

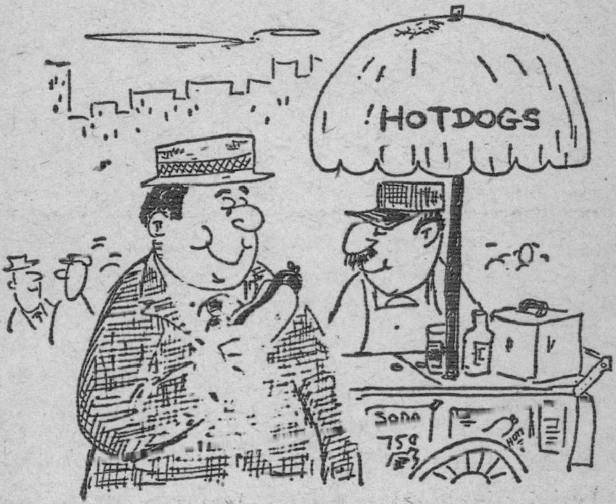
HOTDOGS
SODA
75¢

If an ear of corn and a cabbage had a race, who would win?
The cabbage because it's a head.

~~~~~~

When George Washington crossed the Delaware River, why did he stand up in the boat?
Because everytime he sat down someone handed him an oar.

Why is a snake smart?
Because you can't pull his leg.

~~~~~~

Which month has 28 days?
All of them.

What did Count Dracula want to do on the baseball team?
He wanted to be the batboy.

~~~~~~

How far can you go into a forest?
Half way, then you're coming out.

What did Ringo Starr's father say when he first learned that his son wanted to play the drums?
"Beat it."

~~~~~~

Why do elephants drink?
To forget.

What color is a burp?
Burple.

~~~~~~

What is green and has four legs and a trunk?
A frog on a vacation.

What has 10 legs and shoots a lot?
A basketball team.

~~~~~~

Why did they arrest the baseball player?
Because he was caught stealing bases.

What did one eye say to the other?
"Just between you and me, there is something that smells."

~~~~~~

Why did the city boy go to the country?
He wanted to see a barn dance.

What time is it when a clock strikes thirteen?
Time to get a new clock.

~~~~~~

What kind of shoes does a bum like best?
Loafers.

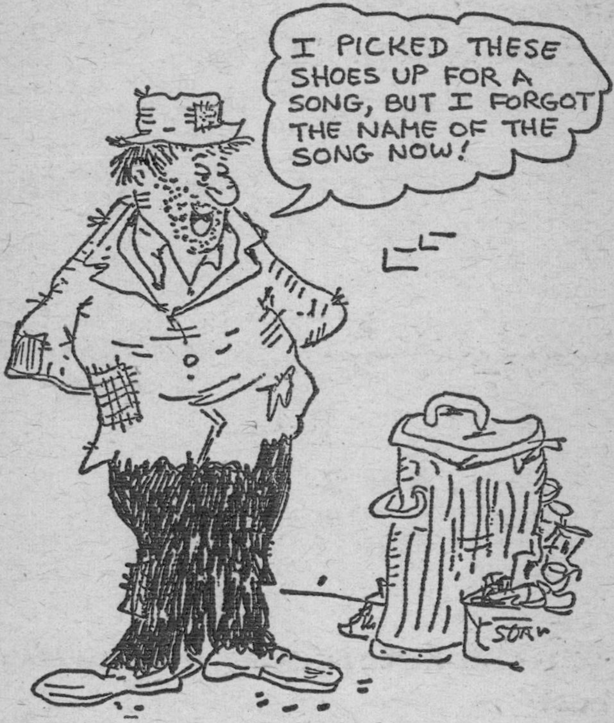
I PICKED THESE SHOES UP FOR A SONG, BUT I FORGOT THE NAME OF THE SONG NOW!

What did the robot say when he ran out of electricity?
"AC come, AC go."

~~~~~~

What did the adding machine say to the secretary?
"You can count on me."

Why did the tough kid put his father in the refrigerator?
He wanted an ice cold pop.

～～～～～～～～～～～～～～～～～～～～～～～～～～

What was the biggest operation?
Lansing, Michigan.

What is the best way to raise cabbage?
With a knife and fork.

What has a lot of problems?
A math book.

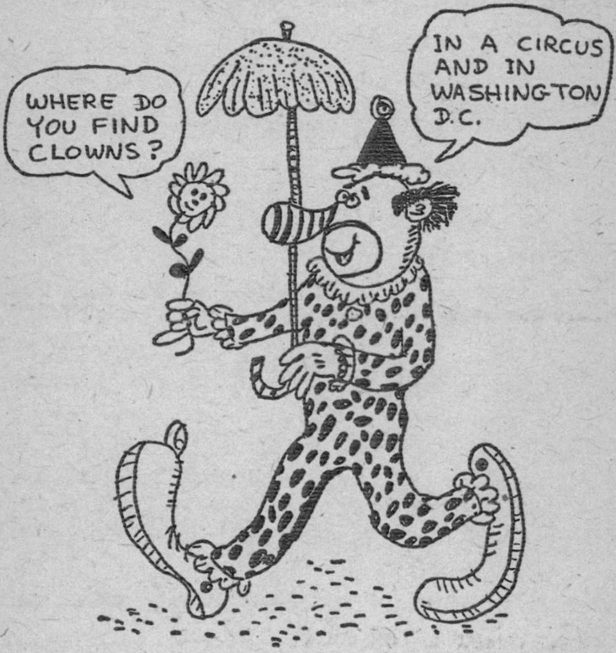
WHERE DO YOU FIND CLOWNS?
IN A CIRCUS AND IN WASHINGTON D.C.

What's yellow and goes up and down?
A banana in an elevator.

~~~~~~

Name seven things that contain milk.
A milkshake and six cows.

What do you call a smart duck?
A wise quacker.

~~~~~~

What's red and writes under water?
A ballpoint apple.

What do you call a zookeeper?
A critter sitter.

~~~~~~

What do you call a car that runs on chicken fat?
A Cacklac.

What do you have when you feed a cat lemonade?
A sour puss.

~~~~~~

What is the best way to avoid falling hair?
Jump back real fast.

Why do birds fly south in the winter?
Because they don't have money for a train ticket.

~~~~~~

Where does Superman get a haircut?
On the top of his head.

What is the best thing to keep hair in?
A cigar box.

~~~~~~

What has six legs and lives in the Himalayas?
The Abominable Pool Table.

What is purple and does magic tricks?
The Grape Houdini.

What happens if you toss a brown stone into the Blue Danube?
It gets wet.

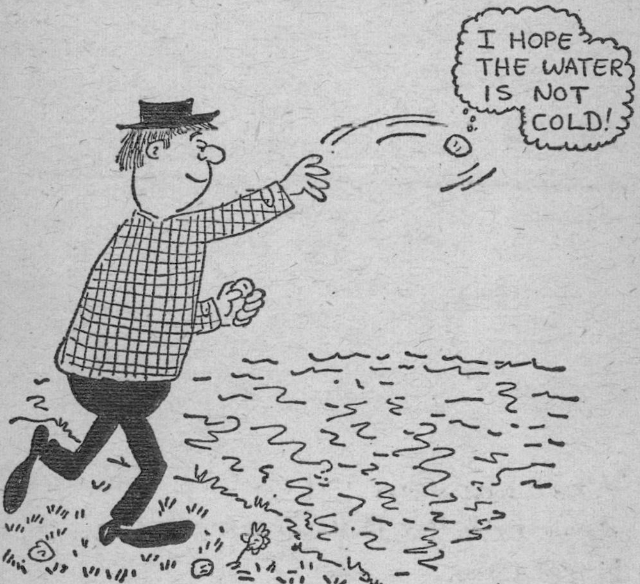
I HOPE THE WATER IS NOT COLD!

How can you make a meat loaf?
Give it a week off.

~~~~~~

What is a tricycle?
A tot rod.

Where does an oyster sue for damages?
Small clams court.

FUN & GAMES FROM WARNER BOOKS

LOTS OF SUPERMAN
BOOKS AND GAMES

SUPERMAN: LAST SON OF KRYPTON
by Elliot S. Maggin   (U82-319, $2.25)
A tiny space ship leaves the dying planet Krypton, carrying the infant
who will become Earth's Superman. Here's the enthralling tale of his
childhood in Smallville, his emergence as newsman Clark Kent, his
battles with archenemy Luthor. It's the one and only original story.

SUPERMAN: MIRACLE MONDAY
by Elliot S. Maggin   (U91-196, $2.50)
The "Man of Steel" meets a demon of fire. C. W. Saturn strikes at the
heart of civilization—but the devastation of the world is not his goal,
only his means to the corruption of the last Kryptonian, the super-
hero who has been stripped of his Clark Kent alias.

SUPERMAN AND SPIDER-MAN
by Jim Shooter, John Buscema & Joe Sinnott   (U91-757, $2.50)
For the first time in paperback form, the two great heroes are united
in an incredible adventure—all in terrific color.

SUPERMAN BLUEPRINTS
                                       (U87-819, $6.95)
A complete set of 15 authentic blueprints of rockets, the star ship,
Luthor's lair, the Fortress of Solitude, Jor-El's laboratory, Hoover
Dam, the trial arena, Krypton City. Every scene is laid out to scale in
exact size. Each drawing is 13⅛x19 inches. Includes a beautifully-
designed plastic carrying case.

SUPERMAN CUT-OUTS
by John Harrington & Aldo Cappelli   (U97-068, $7.95)
The diorama you make yourself. Just cut, color, paste, and assem-
ble using ordinary household glue, scissors and coloring materials.
Features three action sets from the movie, including scenes from
Krypton, Kansas and Metropolis. Over eighty pieces in all and hours
of fun.

SUPERMAN PORTFOLIO
by Jim Dietz   (U87-821, $7.95)
Only today's awesome technology could translate Superman to the
screen. Only a superlative artist could capture the impact of the
motion picture. Jim Dietz is that artist and these original paintings,
commissioned exclusively for this portfolio, provide an enduring
memory. All suitable for framing.

GREAT TRIVIA BOOKS
FROM WARNER BOOKS